I0110727

Metropole

Metropole

Ken Bolton

PUNCHER & WATTMANN

© Ken Bolton 2024

This book is copyright. Apart from any fair dealing for the purposes of study and research, criticism, review or as otherwise permitted under the Copyright Act, no part may be reproduced by any process without written permission. Inquiries should be made to the publisher.

First published in 2024
Published by Puncher & Wattmann
PO Box 279
Waratah NSW 2298

info@puncherandwattmann.com

**NATIONAL
LIBRARY**
OF AUSTRALIA

A catologue record for this book is available from The National Library of Australia.

ISBN   9781923099425

Cover design by Ken Bolton

Printed by Lightning Source International

Some of these poems have been published previously:
'Dude—(lunch in the slow time of the year)' in *No Placebos*
'Ben Sando Ode' in *Rabbit*
'For Giorgio de Chirico' in *Shearsman* (UK) and *Best Australian Poems*
'('If you take requests') The Stars, a cosmology' in *No Placebos*
'Swimmeroonie' in *Saltbush Journal*
'Midwinter Day' in *Otoliths* and *Best Australian Poems*
'Oh Boy Bear and Berrigan (or 'Yeti Four')' in *Saltbush Journal*
and 'Night Thoughts' in *Overland*

Many thanks to the editors

Thanks, too, to friends who have read this work
Pam Brown, Laurie Duggan, Peter Bakowski, Kai Jensen and John Levy

Contents

Dude!—(lunch in the slow time of the year)   9

Ben Sando Ode   13

For Giorgio De Chirico   20

('If you take requests') The Stars, a cosmology   22

Swimmeroonie   32

New Tunes   35

•

Kate   52

Midwinter Day   62

A Misty Day in Late July, 2020   67

Oh Boy Bear and Berrigan (or 'Yeti Four')   82

•

The Metropole Poems

An Australian Afternoon—Faces at The Metropole   93

Night Thoughts   109

An Unsuitable Attachment   131

•

Cath & Pontoon at Horseshoe Bay   147

•

Notes   151

Dude!—(Lunch, In The Slow Time Of The Year)

for Danny & Hayley

awake & refreshed
—tho with nothing on the page
—Pam Brown

"I was looking for that,"
Danny says & picks up his rag

Leaving me

Neither awake

nor refreshed

Tho with 'nothing on the
page'

—Which is usual—

but a
coffee
Which is expected, & is
"something to be going on with," as
a teacher I once had used to say,

as he ducked out the classroom, the

implication, hanging in the air,

that a clip over the ear was in waiting

on his return—if called for. He

also used the expression "reading matter"

which I resented—as I resented

him, pretty much

                      But the coffee's okay.

As is the waiter

                  At any rate

"Okay by me"

                Danny finishes polishing

the last table, moves behind the counter.

A girl goes by, chuffed to be on her

dad's shoulders—perhaps seven, maybe

eight years of age. Her mum walks

by her young husband's side.

They have 'done their bit'

                    —for *this* poem—

& are gone,

              "leaving me (etcetera)—"

but with something on the page.

Enough?
Not enough, probably. And this is not
the part of town—*out of term*—
to assist with the poem.

Looking out the window
only cars go by, the cafe is empty.

The students
who loll

—over beers,

lattes—

are weeks away.

One sometimes hears
an enlivening phrase from them.
Études, dude—hey!

No, nothing like, but they
can be amusing—

or staggeringly depressing

(along the "reading matter" lines)—

depending what you hear.

Some phrases I love.

"Better than a
poke in the eye with a burnt stick"
I always liked. You don't hear it now.

I remember Forbes said it once,
of something—a rejection letter? an
acceptance?
                    (I don't mean his heart—
a poem being accepted, or rejected. Who rejected
John's poems?)

                    Ah, lunchtime! & I
so look forward to you. Why?

Ben Sando Ode

                                        "My dream a drink
                    with Ira Hayes
                                        we discuss the code of the west"
                                        — Ted Berrigan, *The Sonnets*

                                Then,

I walk out in the village

                    & look for you.

                Now
it is Ted Berrigan I quote

                    #

                                (MEANWHILE)

        I wonder how Ben is going

                            I mean "with them"?

                    #

        the paintings
                        #
                                "I,

red-faced

        & romping in the wind"

Absence of passion, principles, love

                (&)

                    I

never place things right, never win

             "You are asleep
A lovely light is singing to itself"
             "Red-faced &
romping in the wind"   —

         Yes how does he go?

Cap'n Aubrey, now
     he goes about, setting up ship

               (A matter
of endless delay)

       How strange to be gone in a minute

Aubrey never is.

I will be. One day. That day

is a long way off

A long, long way?

"A cast-off

emotion"

One John I think used somewhere

a 'tough' idea

he'd have loved

— been attracted to,

approving *of* —

And who is

Ira Hayes,

that we should discuss it with him

the code

of the West?

"Then, I walk out in the bleak village

& look for you"

you are fixing a tyre, painting a chair

or something

achieving normalcy

casually, like

a knack

"Hullo, Ira."

You smile.

        It is a great smile, wide.

                I guess

You may have had

        'a position on this'?

            But the West

would never care.

      An anomaly

         'statistically not signifcant'.

             (But as
             who isn't,

'finally'?)

Which code had Ted meant,
America's? or the later, *post-war* West's?

The same code, either way—
'Get The Money!'

        #

Pam's last poem

not her last ever,

her most recent—

very French & sunny

Cendrars, Queneau,   Peret?

#

I look up

("Hi, folks!")

take in

BIZARRE ATTEMPTS

AT NORMALCY

Leigh Street

#

four bizarre attempts—

• a guy, in slightly too tight suit, brief-case etc—suit

too shiny—walks past, long face, tanned, jowly,

(the suit sky-blue),

looking like a Central American politician

('of' the right)

Fernando Rey

"never place things right,
      never win"

                    Resembling the author of *Paroles*
                          (Prevert) ?

bizarre attempts—

• girl & guy, girl anxious, gauging things:
                          her presentability;
obstacles etcetera; hair from face; how jacket hangs; *he*,
looking at the ground ruminative

                    • Two interestingly different,
yet linked, companions —on-the-grift— faces that frown, & scowl,
menacing—on the look-out, no expectation—tanned—*he*
Anglo maybe, the friend Islander

                    • how I hate a hoodie—
dressed for unexceptionability
            anonymity, in-
                  visible
                    the colourless middle class

am *I* not middle class,

                  colourless?   Often,

not today.

            • An idiot with an 'Australia pin' (gold)

on his suit

            Liberal Party?

                    fool, merely?

                #

                      Ah, Ben Sando —

where are you, now?   in the ring —

                like Ted

            when the bell rings

                          ('?')

facing off

        against THE GREAT BUT

                ABSENT ART OF OUR AGE

                (?)

                  Place things right,

win!

For Giorgio De Chirico

Hang it all, Giorgio,

there is only the one battered faucet—

pouring out the ongoing present, in the minutes we possess.

Unstoppable. There is no rest.

Whether you live in Rome or Port Elliot,

there is none. Better than living in Dorset. All three tho

bring, to my mind, calm. Rome's traffic,

necessarily, *compels you to seek it*—a darkened room, a quiet square.

      Port Elliot suggests a certain

melancholy—but restful. And Dorset? a boarding house, a curtain

pulled against the drear sea view, the esplanade malefic—

& *empty*: dour sea wall, where lamp posts, regularly spaced,

make their unconvincing case for the decorative;

the sea itself—& the sky, just barely differentiated

from the water beneath. Time, here, is exterminated, greyed,

denied purpose. One would turn inside to a television—if

in Dorset. Let us not—in any sense of the term—

go there (*& in fact I've never been*, nor you,

Giorgio). We confine ourselves to Rome—

& Port Elliot, with its fine beach. In the town's South Seas bookshop

      a tome

devoted to your work sits, has sat for a year or more—for you to purchase, or to rummage thru—looking for the good ones.

Ha, ha, ha. My joke. They're *all* good

one way or another. I've been thru it many times, as must have others.

(It continues to look … *'fresh'.* 'Ish'.) The loopy ones I sort of covet …

But I have a lot at home—many a book

with works by *you*, Giorgio. My most enduring

enthusiasm. You set me on the road to loving paintings.

You, & one or two others, whom I've forgotten. ('Relegated'.)

(Nolde, Ensor.) *Then* how did it go? Munch; the contemplative

yet intense Cezanne; Matisse & Picasso—their unremitting

& inventive purpose; the great of the past—Rembrandt, Velazquesz,

Piero & Titian. The Baroque, the Rococo. My hero

Manet, & so on … Pollock. And

—who have I left out?—Kirchner, Beckmann,

… (Rauschenberg). The *minor* greats—Marquet, Filippo

de Pisis. And, 'Now'. (… Oehlen, Christopher Wool.) Time

does not stand still. The faucet again. Where the element plunges out

in terrifying chunks, heavy with implication—*of your making.*

Timeless & urgent. I could *stand* beside that faucet—

lounge—metaphysical, yes—like the guy in the drawing, *The Mysterious*
Baths.

Don't make me revisit Dorset—Bournemouth, Weymouth—I couldn't.

('If You Take Requests')—The Stars, A Cosmology

"So, Mister—Mister DJ—keep those records spinning"

(for Lou, Patti, Thelma, the Christines)

The Thelmas

\#

(& there is Seneca, of course,

     the property tho

of Thomas 'Sphere' Eliot)

    \#

The Pleiades

The wisdom of Jimmy Barnes

      —wide, comprehending—

("I'd die to be
with you tonight")

       \#

tho " *JIMMY LIVES!* "

(old saying)

#

from the night sky

the Thelmas

look down

stellar twins

kindly divinities

wise, consolatory

they do not forgive

they do not forget

they accept

#

here I sit

on this bench,

(stile almost),

(simple 'form') —

    & gaze out —

    upon the round slope,

    of the hill, as it falls away—

    sered grass, the limbs &

    stems of the gums—('die-back')—

    to the vast pond of blue

                Kangaroo Island

\#

blue   orange   silver

\#

         where I lived once

for a week

•

the Christines

•

Irwin & O'Connor

The Caths

Catherine Murphy, Cath Cantlon

Dejection? an Ode?

"(O)des" — think Keats

O'Hara, Pindar

would Adorno figure,

here, amongst these tutelary

figures?

The Johns — (Forbes & Jenkins) —

& Glenn Johns

The Thelmas,

(Ritter & Todd)

who
look down judiciously

With some pity? some
gesture
... of acknowledgement ?

— Mistakes,
Errors Of Judgement —

(Thelma warned of them

suffered *for* them)

To dance, to
hot cha-cha

& die

                              expire upon

                              a car seat in

                              a garage the

                              motor running

        wearing a boa

                    The dead Ted

                    & O'Hara

                    we who are about to hot cha-cha ...
                                    etcetera

    John Barbour

                Freddy King.

                                        MONTY!

                (Rommel ??)

                                    Montgomery Clift

(though

        was he

                                                27

a

"Young Lion"

technically ?)

who might have played him,
in the bio pic we will never have

the live a-hunted
& the dead a-huntin'

[O'Hara]

JOHN — & his "luminous hum"

we/I salute him

and the hornet
Jimmy chased from the room
outside

to some "various field"

the stars, that look *down*

protectively

On me, on Catherine

no, not

the city,

(near Darwin, Alice Springs)

Cath Kenneally

that look down, maybe,
on Tony Towle

that look down,

at least, 'in' him

— tho where? in which?

in some, surely —

as he goes
to Bloomingdales

On Pam & Jane,

the stars look down

on Rosemary & Laurie

on Banana & Chris

& Gabe & Stacey

on Yuri, on Yuki

& Tengis & Gerel

on Noah,   & Teague & Jude & Ryder

Clinton!

Clinton Kenneally—
(not George, not Bill)

all is forgiven

Thelma Ritter, look after them

Give them some good times   (Lou, Patti Smith, Thelma Todd ...

((Sam Cooke))

...   )

#

Play that song called 'Soul Twist'

Swimmeroonie

for and after Harry Mathews

I had always wanted to be 'the Swimmer' (de Chirico's "Swimmer") &,
Pleased with the morning weather, dove—
I would cross the Pacific by myself. Neither she,
      nor I, nor the Williamstown refineries, minded.

Still so near. *Must swim harder.* Love's birthday (& here
Her form is recollected: *gold* on sheets of *red*), a day on which
Are nullified all crimes of the then future.
(And the now past's? Forgotten.)
In this striking out—for clarity, for definition—
      momentary innocence is corseted.

To not be blamed, be guiltless, *have*, at least,
Occupation. Yet the swimmer's back, though it signals
"No can answer!", does presuppose
      a querying of purpose: responsibilities,
      dart-like, find it,

Its attractive liberty. To continue or return!
To succeed—*or not to fail?* Is that a question?
& all is invalidated. Think? Or swim?
      On the pier figures wonder. *Or,*
      perhaps, don't (spit, buy sandwiches, smoke, feed gulls).

A useful violence strengthens shoulders, back, biceps.
With no gift to beguile, I must exhaust them or me,
Float in the shadows of waves, spouting—
        thinking thoughts of a 'pissed-off' nature,
        committed, now, to *arrival*.

What was I committed to before? 'Leaving'?
I'm not leaving again!—*I will have just got here!*
Thoughts like these do that beguiling
        I could not imagine: *I dream idly*, for example,
        of the Futurist paintings—
"Those Who Leave", "Those Who Stay", by Boccioni—
& plough the waves, arms forgotten, a leaver.

"One false moof & I die you," I cry, "you bunth
Of bathtards!", combining *i scrittori* Koch & Kerouac—
Bitterly, manic—laughing, at the very inappropriateness.
        A gull passes—rude
        & abstract, limbs fatten, &,

Winsome with particularity, a gulp of brine
Crudely drives me on, an old car made sound—
By virtue of panic—speaking loudly to my knees, my arms, &
        Shoulders, which recombine in darkness—
To smite with iron the iron sea. (To not drown!)
        (To not go under!) And,

voluptuous pronouncements of decease behind,
I swim, a swimmer, a swimmeroonie! Yet arrival

Comes to seem like 'No Departure'.
My companions, the sky & whitecaps, 'are mine', familiar. And brine.
    The sand is mine.
    And understanding of my life
... shrinks, wrong, to the merely handiest
       What, me worry? "Shall I sit over here?"
       & a towel is handed ... "Well swum,

Whacker!"—the conductor, a bit-part player
From *Lucky Jim* (busless, I see
But fully in uniform,
       down to money-pouch, tickets...)—
       speaking, thrusts a towel at me.

    I take it.

    That is how I left Sydney for Adelaide,
    & started over.

New Tunes — The Breakfast Of Champions

1 PLAY!

All new tunes on the jukebox

but actually I've gone back
to the old:

reading Ted.
'Everybody's
In The Mood'
says Wolf

          (Mood, mood, mood)

the washing's out.
Coffee's on the stove,

           the dog
has gone to her favourite chair

Big Voice Odom:
gonna build himself a

spaceship—fly up to the moon.
Where am I going with this ! ?

(Who's going anywhere?)

("Ain't goin' move"
Johnny Guitar Watson)

I read 'Peace', 'Tulsa Song',
'Heroin', 'American Express'

& I am *there* again
—*where I've never been*—

except with those poems:

alive, the sun coming up

cold rosy dawn
& New York skyline,

docks, the Brooklyn Bridge
(Williamsburg—is it?), as if

Jane Freilicher
Fairfield Porter

painted them

I should ring Tony Towle
but he would be in bed

at this hour
whatever hour it is

?

dawn in the poem,
mid morning here

evening in New York (!)

What to say —
"I'm drunk, with no clothes on!"

  (as someone says
in a poem of Ted's)?

Tho I'm dressed.

The last thing Tony needs
is a prank call

"Bluebird, bluebird,"
says Wolf, "I'm just as lonely

as a man can be."

Not me. Not Wolf either
he sounds happy

My poor heart
keeps on cryin'. Baby, you

so far, far away

(Jimmy
Liggins)

& the sax boots in.
Jimmy who recorded

'Drunk'.
tho he mostly recorded sober

#

Ray

"You crazy, Ray!"
(Mme Dufrene)

A marked man—
Roussel can't have had

many mornings like this one.
Were they 'available' then—did Manet

start a slow day
sometimes,

with coffee, Wolf & a little
poem? Did

Cendrars, Gus Moreau?

2
INFORMATION

The wonderful bleakness
in Memphis Minnie —

"and left me
with a broken heart"

Liggins — a failed career
of great songs

Big Voice Odom
called sometimes 'Voice' Odom

mostly a second string rhythm guitar
but great

great finally, on record,
singing for Jimmy Dawkins.

Mister Moon Man,
can I come up & stay with you?

#

Sykes —
they called him 'Keg'.

3
BREAKFAST OF CHAMPIONS

Manet was 'no angel'.

(Tho we like him.)
And he died young because of it.

(One theory.
Or 'the sins of the father', another.)

So, what he had
for breakfast
after a big night

—or on a deliberately
slow day

—an early but slow start—

on a picnic
with his wife—

(I wonder what their life
was 'like')

A picnic with—this day, maybe—
some painting thrown in.

        —Coffee?
tea? eggs — *scrambled*, say.

A hero of mine
(a century & a half

too late for it to matter, for him,
or show originality on my part)

it is hard to put your finger on

'exactly what it is'
that makes the great ones so incisive

so deliberate,

so unassailably complete as gestures—

the picnic on the grass,
Olympia with her cat & servant,

the same model years later
before the iron fence & the

railway station. Her daughter holding
the bars & peering thru—(her

young back to us)—at the steam
surrounding the train,

her mother's frank gaze
(the usual term), her seeing

but thoughtful eyes;
the still-lives (flowers,

sometimes only one or two,
in glass, or simple vase).

So we know intelligence
was part of his personality

what else do we know?

(Charm, good-naturedness
a nice enough guy —

& the stories about
'wanting acclaim'—so?)

•

Cendrars — is of the century
I've lived mostly in,

so, no top hats, a less
class-bound system

of government—
tho of course

we can suppose this
& only be wrong

—*our* wearing jeans & staying poor
is not like his —

Cendrars has a hair-
of-the-dog for all I know

& three or four Gitanes
or Gauloises

& a sausage
cold from the ice-box

He dips it once or twice
in a pool of tomato sauce

& goes out the door, humming.

He has one arm,
he hasn't shaved &

considers going for a haircut

—a Friday, so why not?

Gustave
Moreau

older than Manet

born earlier
& outliving him too. Cold,

a little brittle, upper class,
gay, tho he'd have kept it quiet

(& as I've done nothing brave in my life
I cannot judge)

an eccentric, who backed the
wrong horse stylistically, in the

art stakes: idealist, symbolist,
away with the fairies
                            Baudelaire's
remarks, about the ludicrousness
of paintings of people

in helmets & togas —
shields & sandals —

& his call for *the heroism*
of modern day life

— (the business suit, the
hat, & shoes & polish) —

made the case.

Yet the teenager
of every generation

will find Moreau,
at least briefly, fascinating

like Sci Fi Fantasy.

He lived to formally teach
some of the Fauves,

a fact I like

tho how much attention
they paid we'll never know.

(Matisse thought Moreau
'lacked courage'.)

One of the Fauves I like least—
for his subject matter, & his religiosity—

did a portrait of Gustave
I care about: it shows

a modern, moustachioed
head & bowler hat
                        —almost
as if prescribed
by the strictures of Baudelaire

(an irony, or
time's revenge)—

& has the face
slightly flattened & therefore modern,

almost cubist—
or as if in deference to Cubism.

So there he is,
caught by a

not unsympathetic

not unkind

later age

in the idiom of a later time.

#

(Rouault's portrait.)

#

I don't think Moreau

had big nights

—except nights of work—

& so for breakfast?

I don't know, melon?

tea & toast

lemon juice?

—— something cleansing & asperative

or purgative.

People focus too much on the life,

rather than read the books, of Roussel —

& it is hard not to

(tho I read *New Impressions*

a few months ago,
& I read him now)

Probably an awful life

—bizarre, we know—the money
(no shirt worn twice, etc etc), the

madness &
delusions.

Unhappy, he himself said.

Distraction,
& hard work

& not much communing with
anyone.
     Suicide finally.

But the work is
extraordinary
     teenage, & yet extraordinary:
just extreme and weird &
funny & beautiful

curiously moving

& curiously *curious.*

For breakfast?

Uppers & downers.

Did he meet Moreau?

What would

that be like,

each regarding the other

as *outré,* irrelevant—

Moreau uncomfortable at speaking

to this nutter,

Roussel uncomfortable

because he was Roussel,

& there was no one to turn to

after the death of his sister.

A loner.

Pills.

And for Victorine Meurent,

(Manet's model

& herself a painter, & not,

probably, a bohemian

—too smart—

a mother?)

Something sensible.

What she thought of them

we might wonder.

Some notes

Sykes—Roosevelt Sykes, to give him his full name.

Blaise Cendrars lost an arm in WW1.

In fact we do know about Moreau's teaching of the Fauves—the younger
artists liked Moreau. Matisse though, finally held that Moreau was afraid
to back his more progressive students.

The portrait of Moreau: When was it made, *after* his death?

The facts about Manet are not clear. The painting described features
artist & model Victorine Meurent, with, perhaps, her daughter, but staged
anyway so as to appear a governess in the painting—or a mother—her
clothes might be taken not to indicate 'servant'. Meurent herself painted.

Kate

What's 'arvo' for morning, says Pam's poem
an evocation ... of self-conscious Australian
complacency,

        barefooted ease.

Here — Cath, Allan, Linda, me —
at Marion Bay,

        a less summery feel

Clear autumn skies—which I describe
for friend John Levy
partly because, typing—on the
small phone—slows one, to just that pace
where the words shuffle themselves into
measured & communicative order

        'Lowell' ?

I am surprised Linda doesn't know
— never heard of him. But why
should she, a musicologist? The Art Gallery
of South Australia's director
apparently thought the 'man in the street'

—ordinary people—

would know Louis Buvelot for example.

('Bubbles'.)

('Bubbles' Buvelot?)

Why should they?   I am explaining
Elizabeth Hardwick —

reading her again—*Sleepless Nights*—my fourth
my fifth time.
So I've read a lot more of her than of him.
I like his translations of Leopardi
& not much else.

Kate Jennings has died

(Their 'New York' intellectual style
—too late tho—Kate—for *The Partisan Review*—
but dry, mandarin, sharply intelligent;

judgements & distinctions like—
that *were* in fact?—demonstrations of difference, superiority

admonishments, that were
complacently, or securely,
self-regarding (?) Like knowing the right
cutlery, like not being soft
self election to a minority, the correct.)

(I began that, I think, as a question.)

I met her a few times, we spoke,
I did not know her really. She came
to our parties, knew my name for a sec.

Actually—then—she was the lone subject of her life
intense, a celebrity poet maudite—fragile,
admired, feared for.

And straightened out.

A tale she tells herself. I like her poem
for Martin Johnston—a lot—tho its play
for the high ground is funny. But
even so.

I hum a little Billie Holiday

& stop—in case I have hummed those lines
too often—at various junctures across

the morning, annoying maybe
to Linda (a musicologist)

Arlo, amusingly (aged three?)

rather likes Billie Holiday—'What a Little
Moonlight Can Do', 'It's Too Hot For Words'
'What a Night, What a Moon, What a Boy'

#

Australia killed Martin Johnston, because we're
all alcoholics.

#

Tho I never bought Martin a drink,
while Kate may have. Anyway.
Do I want to talk about any of these
things?—Death, fragility, ageing,
failure;
insights, suicide ? (Jazz?)—

or do I just want to talk,
late morning / early-arvo style
because, 'aeolian', I seem
'open to suggestion'? the clouds, lying

one moment flat above the sea's horizon,

then massing, bright

but freighted with a reserve of grey
—the controlled burn-off of days ago—

over the sea.

                              Cath
comes in & there is discussion—of the beach, birds, trails:

A steep path down, but do-able; *a guinea fowl?*
pretty anyway; the sand, *soft*—& a good stretch
of cushion-soft seaweed

                              Kate achieved a style,
one of clarity

perhaps a distrustful one: down
on herself, unimpressed—hence
the impatience with others
(the self-forgiving—*arvo time*,
barefoot, weekender—'easy'
take on things)

but high, 'sure' sophistication :

deft, casual, *adamant.*

And recrimination & self-distaste
a bitter corrective, scolding.

Adam Ant — ha-ha — who, today,
remembers him? (Kate's two lone albums
when one saw her flat—Roy Orbison *Ballads*
& Brenda Lee. Her book *Come to me
my Melancholy Baby*)

we must learn what Kate has learned,

& know she has learned it—
better than us, that she is transformed
('corrected') while we remain … Australian?

You are a herd,
that I have left

Did she mean to say those things

—and am I conflating the two—Elizabeth & Kate?—

or was it a performance, a trying on
of clothes—dressing-up—
a camouflage ?

                        #

I guess we're 'all'
                    for self-improvement.

(Kris Hemensley tells the man beside him
 he is English, not Australian,
 & the man beside offers, *Couldn't he
 aspire at least?* The bar. Alcohol again.)

                        #

Elizabeth Hardwick's sympathy could feel like
no sympathy — dry-eyed, exacting, all-seeing.
Observed, not personal.

"It is time for cocktails," says Hardwick. "The
moment for which all of New York
works, lies, exercises, hurries, dresses."

Is that where you would go
to kick the habit?

But—a change of scene—
it worked for Kate

Martin's parents drank, 'a lot', getting Martin started
at an early age. So it wasn't 'Australia'. Except—
they were Australian.

#

                    Is there something shameful
about travelling to the Centre

to become one of them, take on
their strength?

("I made it in New York" ... you little people)

To be metropolitan, above error
endorsed

The point is — a point is — why am I saying
these things about Kate?

                    is it because
she didn't need my approval?

Exemplary,

       & prepared to be lonely

her loneliness, for her
the human condition

As an individual she spoke to 'us'
who made her so—

addressed 'individually'
as a plural—a mob—a herd, a crowd.

guilty, lesser, ignorant, faulty

          #

Feminism was suddenly a going concern
after Kate Jennings & so was Women's Poetry

Look upon my works, ye mighty ...

Kate achieved things—& got out.

We were the grudging crowd.
She was right to leave

escaped being tagged forever, made to answer regularly—
"How do you feel now, Kate, ten, twenty, fifty years on?"
"Do you still ...... ?" Etcetera.

#

"Kate Jennings, you will have a position on this."

#

Made a stock figure, diminished,
prisoner of a great moment. Put back in her box.

She got out. Went there,
made a life.

#

I write this, look out the window at
the clouds again, try to recall her

Midwinter Day

off to pick up Noah

a lift?   No

I walk, hands in pockets, shoulders hunched

   in the sun

   made to feel   like James Dean
         in a famous picture

     consequently, handsomer, too
         tho I don't imagine

I really am

I'm whistling
   a tune I whistle a lot

   tho what is it exactly

   early Wayne Shorter

I say hullo to an old lady coming my way
   80 maybe

then what was I thinking about? —

       of *Midwinter Day* ?

                          I read it in 1982

imported direct from Small Press Distribution

tall & blue—dark blue—& the format a little big
so I have always to find a place for it
                    or forget
               —search—
& think, "Must've lent it to someone"
                         — "And I know
just whom."
         Then months later see it again
or 'years later' it seems

               had I given it to Ann
in a fit of niceness
        self-renunciation?
                  Not me,
as it turns out
         There it is.   Have I ever

actually, finished it?

I know the first pages well,

but I

have

no memory of its end

Bits of Alice's podcast

make it seem unfamiliar

So maybe not.

Up on the main road, across from the school
it's mostly guys—usually plenty of mums—to
pick up the kids

who mass soon, at the lights
in small groups of twenty or so—on foot, on
bikes—& a mum or dad or two between. Noah
is always in the third batch.

The tune is
'Moon of Manakoora'

I walk a street or two & turn, where the new place is going up
enormous slab, piles & racks of wood, ready, waiting, ready to go

then up Cumberland beside the oval to the main road, & left
to the traffic lights—offered a lift by another parent starting out

but I prefer to walk

     #

as I said, unaccountably jaunty

   — (the song) —

tho no red jacket
or Jimmy's face so photogenic

     #

Turns out I don't know the beginning either—
but the section further on where she talks about
people, the others all about her, I know.

And later there's that good patch
where she lists everything—every thing
she does, incidents, chores, difficulties,
interruptions—memories—then every business or building
in the small American town, a tour.

Large parts of the poem are on target
Larger parts are not. The dreams, the default
reliance on beads & feathers & mythology
that isn't hers. *Midwinter Day* makes its point,
signals its type well—but muffs the execution.
Making Mayer exemplary as an experimentalist,
she proves her point: '*This* could be done.'
but not such a good poet: large parts are dull—

the standard American regard for dreams and analysis—as in "Georgette's analyst says..." —to no real end. Almost like superstition. The archetypes.

"Hullo, Noah. How was it today?"

A Misty Day In Late July, 2020

> "Dark grey, diminished, chipped, and soiled,
>   the city seemed a scale model of its former self,
>   a wintry film in black-and-white."

The mist hangs outside at a height of
six to ten feet, prettily blanketing houses & trees.

The streets around vaguely story-book, wistful, enchanting:
grey, blue-grey—how lyrical can this be,

a grey day?

Paris: a down-at-heel intersection, of two
small streets—

                        gutters,
unpeopled footpaths.   Cobblestones;

the back mudguard of a Citroen, departing. ('WWII'—
packaging, signage, conceding no date.)

                                A photo,
colourless, monochrome.

                    In
Adelaide, people seem
cautious, caution*ing*——

but aware——the common
plight acknowledged——

nicer to each other.

          #
My mind moves
to the fog in *Maigret.*
          #

                         While
I like them, people are less
interesting to watch so self-aware.

Observing them one sees only

the same thing: a narrowed range
of behaviours.

                    The mist
is slightly spooky——or 'quotes' it.
There is no threat: before the fences

are trees the wisps of mist furl &
twist around—suggesting *'follow'*

more than *'beware'*. Some enchantment.

You couldn't see across the oval, says Cath
who has disappeared into it—a walk—

& returned, hair a little damp.

Noah's birthday. Seven. We take presents across
(& one for younger brother, Arlo—a

'bee' suit—so he will not feel left out).

Later, Max & Finn call in—tea & scones
with their mum, while they play. Finn,

one-&-a-half, offers me a drink in my absence—
lifts a toasting glass to Michael's portrait of me

that hangs in the hall. It doesn't 'look' like me
& yet it does—every kid has recognised it

instantly. Can I look as mean as that
& yet be loved? (Those poor children.)

                    Months ago I wondered
whether this would seem a big event

& now it seems it is
& that it will seem so

                              & might see me off
                              (Conceivable)

          #

Conventionally people are thought
unable to imagine they might die

tho they'd concede that they will—
but 'notionally'.

          #

               Why
is my vocabulary so small?
The tiny patterns of my thought

               #

All the 'awareness' — (a long, lengthening phase

of 'psychic surplus', says a journalist)

—are we all getting 'too sensitive'?

I remember that was a joke once—

Unwanted, unrequired—there is

no new data *to warrant it*

> "They have Australian or possibly New Zealand
> accents & they talk to each other in a speedy
> technical patois. They tell me to collect my things
> & come down to the ambulance. I put on my scarf
> & jacket, check that I have money, pick up the
> suitcase, & follow them downstairs. At the open door
> L & I embrace hurriedly & with a certain agitation.
> On the pavement, I look back at her, standing in the
> doorway, half silhouetted against the hall light.
> As I wave goodbye, it occurs to me that this is the
> moment when I am to have the thought 'This may be
> the last time I see her'; so, I have that thought, & then,
> like a shadow, it crosses my mind that, if I do die,
> the sharpest poignancy of this moment will be lost on me.
> I walk to the ambulance & get in."

("lost *on* me" or "lost *to* me"?)

Nicholas Spice in the *LRB*—an account of corona virus—

on-top-of-it, unflappable ...

'Going Quietly'? pretending
never to have 'been' flapped.   Null.

#

the poem written to accompany Eleanor's
art work 'has its moments'—tho it's too much

like a review (my writing I notice here, now,
taking on the civilised all-knowingness

of the *LRB* writers—all shock 'absorbed', more
filed than registered, or do they register it

at some 'human' level they then suppress?
everything, always (pre-) dealt with.

"Always already" was a phrase irritating
in the 90s, where it seemed too frequently used 1),

too knowing 2), and 3) an unearned, self-awarded
"I'm smart" badge. A tic, almost, for the *Art & Text* crew,

the catalogue essayists, others. 'Crying out'
for inverted commas.

The poem begins, wondering, at the change
in her art—from slightly jokey minimalist conceptualism

(meaning, for me, Andre, LeWitt, & others
Concrete blocks, variously assembled)—to a

*duelling sword, a fencing foil—& a piece of lightly hanging
draped cloth* (a fine silk, probably)

She sends a drawing; & I like it, & like it
for being what it is, referring 'elsewhere'

(#

Bronia Iwanczak,
                    & Bronwyn Platten

)

                              I always like
artists' drawings—of works, of *ideas* for work—
style sacrificed—it is not the point

#

a drawing of a work of art

not a drawing as a work of art

                #

yet they have style anyhow, while pointing entirely

to idea. Bronny & Bron—*the Brons' Age*—1988?

into the 2000s

Gone.

Bronia, trying to make it in the UK—or Europe

& Bron, in the UK also, but for now, dormant.

('Bronwyn' was always too hard to say—or *got*, anyway,

inevitably shortened. Bronny, Bron, 'the Beeper'

'BP' — the Australian shortening of names

Bronia was always referred to as Bronia, I think

tho face to face she may have been 'Bron'—strange

that I 'don't remember'. Tho it can hardly matter

I've seen Bron every year or so, in London, in

Adelaide, at airports, in Manchester. Cath saw her

in Scotland.

Bronia I haven't seen in a while

#

how lyric can this get?

can it get anywhere at all?

#

On the sound system, in the car, whenever
a certain song comes up there is the image of

Rae Jones, a photo I took nearly 50 years ago
I don't know how it got there. No other image has.

Or how to take it down
tho why would I?

A beautiful picture
for a prospective book, in the alley behind our

share house, in Glebe. We were friends ... & rivals.
But friends. The leader of our gang, a gang

I no longer wanted to be part of, had never
signed up for—so we drifted ...

but friends.

"Hullo, Rae." (Or—"*You?*" I say—surprised.) It is
not even Rae's sort of song—tho did he *like* songs

anyway? Not pop or rock as I recall. Not blues.

Ghostly. ('Pleasantly ghostly')

I sent the photos to him again before he died
I didn't acknowledge that I knew he was (I was not—

especially—supposed to know.) *It would have been
a while*, I said, *since he'd seen them, if he ever had—*

since 1974—& that his wife, his daughter
would be pleased to see them. He said Hi & thanks

& sent a drawing.

We started the plague months on Bruny Island & the movie
it felt like then was *On The Beach*

now it feels like WWII—France, Nazis, the German
Occupation. (Occupied Paris,

or Rennes—or *Rue de la Rennes?* — a dispirited,
embittered populace.)

Or *Maigret.* Black-and-white? Colourized:

grey; blue.
I. e., 'French'—

while *Foyle's War* was grey merely (London),

& *The Sullivans* was a 'healthy' brown-grey:
indicating

'historical' & 'Australia'—their skin pale,
unhealthy, but 'meaty' in the father's case

(him whom I loathed). "The Sullivans"—became
appropriately, a name for Australians

or Anglo types, ... as used by indigenous Aussies ...
or Greeks & Italians (?) Or did the latter

use "Skips"? They did.

I suppose I am one of them

& must die a Sullivan   (a Skip).

True.

But must I die — must I die *yet?*

& now I say, Rick, Rick, you've got
to save me   (Peter Lorre)

Camus' *The Plague* has been selling well,
since the pandemic got started, (or got started 'in

a big way').   And—since then—I think
'Mediterranean France', 'Nice', 'Marseilles'

(& see images of sweeping, empty
coastal roads curving round a bay)

(Matisse might have worked here)

An image based on a mixture of ... what towns? —
Trieste, Wellington, the Cannes of *To Catch A Thief*, Hvar —

an atmosphere,
a scenario

—where a killer might've killed someone,
where women wore high shoulders & calf-length dresses

\#

These will be common references—(*The Plague*,
the old movie)—but unavoidable

\#

There's a drawing I must fix, to send to Mill—
& one to Mary, why not? tiny pictures of a

fictional tourist town—harbour, palms, buildings
in pastel grey, & pinks & yellows; blue sea,

a sail-boat, fishing craft drawn up on the sand

I've to frame them, in tiny pieces of spliced bamboo
vapid, serene, sunny

    \#

& one day will

    \#

         Dufy,
an artist for our time — ? — or Oehlen,

more defeated, braver (?) a more determined,

hardened worker, tho seeking
pleasure just the same.

The West has invented
some great glass-bead games

& I have been a sucker for all of them

Palm trees Rome   is a window, reflected

met a Yeti once, in the pyjama department
of David Jones.

strewth

hullo!

hi, Bear!

YOU'RE NANA?

Is that ARLO

Oh Boy Bear And Berrigan (Or 'Yeti Four')

"I met a Yeti once, in the pyjama department
of David Jones"

here's my bear—a drawing—
& I look at it, where a cartoon bear
greets three people. A small boy:

"Hi, Bear!" he says. Beside him
Cath, in spotted pants, T-shirt top—
"Hullo."

      I'm drawn in, too,

standing behind them, where
the left side of the page
ends — so I don't quite fit.

(Cardigan, jeans, heavy shoes.)
Struth, I say.
      Surprised, the
bear booms — "*You're* 'NANNA' ??" —

& then, "Is that *ARLO*??"
The bear is big, bulky
& carefully drawn—less
'cartoon' than 'toy' bear. Boy,

does he have presence.

My coffee
nearly finished—I see, near the cup,
a small 'bear' biscuit
one hand outstretched, the other

to his face, to yawn, 'meant'
probably, to indicate
eating or imbibing

On the table, by the bear,
Ted Berrigan appears—
(back-cover photo)—

rounded, not unlike the bear,

in a blue shirt (blue
"for going out"—tho he's reclining,
cigarette in mouth

— & reads, I think, the papers)

I'm on to him, lately
—he'd have
                    been pleased to know —
the sonnets, the 'personal' poems

& will read soon 'Tambourine Life'
& be energised

　　#
my plan.
　　#

Arlo asked for the drawing:
a bear,
& so I put him in, with his

grandmother tall beside him.

"*Put yourself in*," said Arlo.
"There's not much room."
"*You'll fit*," they both say

I too am reading the
technical journals—but
'no help'
　　　　　for example
I come out
more comically—

'red-faced'? 'romping in the wind'?

(& I 'go' ...
)

          #

to pick up a Hyundai
from Maugham Thiem
Port Road, Cheltenham

from its 'service'

a morning 'shot to bits'
saved but, by Arlo, Cath, Ted.

"blue-grey turning green"

I never thought it would
come to this.
                    It has.

A coffee, dark & hot—
fabulous reflections
'about' it — (the saucer,

the spoon, the coffee itself) — and,
more diffused, on the table.

                    Where

is Bronwyn Platten these days?
Eleanor Amor?
Shaun, Ben, Crab ? — John Foubister,

doing a nutty painting
beautiful & smirking— paintings
that are funny.

Ben's paintings, that are japes,
formalist, fast, *winning*.

In London somewhere,
smart, thinking,

in Melbourne, I think
 ('smart', 'thinking'),

lying down, a darkened room,
waiting for an arm to mend

Ben rolls the dice
(Bon ton roulet)

Eleanor, dreaming, in
perfect quips, game set match, *et cetera*

#

Only a monkey would read this

says Berrigan

yet he "knew not" of what he spoke

#

Bull's-eye, still — right?

#

Something Ben might have said,
as he painted. Bull's-eye.

Their sometime effect.

The effect
of Kurt's big abstractions

— 'not unlike' —

lyrical, loose, casual

(A SMALL PHOTO OF TED)

"crossing 6th and 1st

at ice-cold 6 a.m."

\#

                                        Bull's-eye, says Ben …

… but he's painting

\#

It's a matter of

what you put in.

\#

(That sound — Ker-CHING!)

\#

Ben Sando

wins again

        stronger than alcohol,

        more great than song

        are my hands shaking

I should know better

BERRIGAN SHUFFLE

Ted returns,
6th and 1st, *ice-cold*
6.09 a.m. He's got
the paper

#

A wattle bird—functional, beautiful design—
lands in the tree — casts about, leaves.

And here I am.

Ted Berrigan

The Metropole Poems

An Australian Afternoon

Night Thoughts

An Unsuitable Attachment

An Australian Afternoon — Faces at the Metropole

I haven't sat here many times

                But all of them pleasant

the *Hotel Metropole*, outside, under awnings, vines

—no, no vines,

          but greenery & awnings—*cover*—

                             at

tables

      — the street,

              traffic roaring by —

with Ben

        Julie & Michael

                Fran maybe

                        Central Market

                      opposite,

across wide, wide Grote Street.

I remember Rosemary one night after I dropped

her off not far from here laughed

              She'd not,

she said, live in a town where you could do a surprise
U-turn at 8 o'clock,

                    she'd go back to London. A

high-achiever academic
                         —but in Sydney no work for her
                              no work in Melbourne

#

This 'is' Australia
                    —if you don't pause a beat
                                      to examine

what that must mean —

                         I like the faces I typically see here

Chinese family—older parents, middle-aged daughter
drinking, smoking, calm
                         They could be gamblers (tho
they look relaxed
                    aside from daughter busy on her
phone)
            Gamblers, or unrelated workers on a break
                                                  two
young guys

—definitely workers-on-a-break—

face each other, wolf food down, laugh

                                                  one, handsome

in the Australian-surfer—or band-member

                                          (from-the-

seventies)—

                                              way

(a blond Steve Bisley

                        'Stork' might be inside,

the Delltones on the juke box.

                              Tranter's died: that requires

parentheses of its own, of course.

                          How

to discuss?)

                    Now a woman smokes opposite,

                                    over wine,

the papers,

              —fifty?—

                    dull-ly red hair pulled back, tied behind

not enough for a bun: dark glasses, cigarette

                                  'poised'

she *and* the cigarette   Cream, with

orange-&-black, thin, snaky shapes over it,

    her blouse,

                black tights beneath

I like her. I like everyone who drinks alone & calmly

Early afternoon

            perhaps it defines it.

                      There was a moment

—the mid 70s— when things he said were treasured

"Head first into the beautiful accident"

                  A friend & I

used love to quote it

we said it countless times

              ((another John))

but I never wanted to write like Tranter.

                    A

leaf lands in my hand

            —*on* it—

                balances,

brown 'maple leaf-looking'

              in the dip formed

between thumb, fore-finger, & biro.

'Death' ? ?   —John would somehow ask

                                 ('contrive' to)—

'or a leaf merely?'

                      The latter.

                                 Of course,

who *did* I want to write like?

                      No one really.

There was writing I liked

                      & I would write like it

to see what I got

              —*myself,* ideally, or notionally—

                          as it turned out

tho did I think about it?

                          if Ben doesn't show up soon

this will become dangerously focused

                              The woman's

                                    gone

the family,

the two guys left ages ago

Tranter was highly regarded by the young in the 70s
(our crowd)

His books *The Blast Area, Crying in Early Infancy*

#

HE WALKED LIKE A GOD AMONG US
which made us wonder, Why is he
doing that?
& laugh & mutter

#

His self-regard, the implied, undisguised
low-estimate of everyone else,
were irksome.

So.   Difficult.

Ben has not showed, (or 'shown'), which causes me to think.
I have mixed up some days—that is, tomorrow is when I
should be here—& should be somewhere else too.

I've double-booked. I send Ben

                              a message, apologising —

& sit here & continue to write. A few more minutes. One of
the Tranter poems I liked most

                    —'The Romans'—

concerned lunch time

                    (or early morning?)

                                        in Sydney.

Hyde Park, I think.

                    (A comparison is made—no, a conceit is
offered—something about the drunks rolling over, on their benches,
its being like the wind explaining things to the leaves: some truth,
some equation.) I told him a number of times I liked it. Some time
in the 2000s.

                              #

"Tho did I think about it" ? ?   Did I think about anything *else?*

I met two Tranters: no sightings in the
80s, or even early 90s possibly,
a little communication tho: around
publishing him in *Otis*; around
the problem of Les Murray
like an engagement with one's

former headmaster: he, masterfully, but
not excitingly —maybe 'authoritatively'?—
hip (but one was hip oneself,
one knew, hip enough, *&* one's
friends) … we viewed Tranter
with respect and reservations

Then there was *Jacket*—an astounding undertaking—
tho I suspect the Americans read mostly themselves
& ignored the southern hemisphere, still it was
good for Australian writing, & good, maybe,
for individual writers.

       As was the archive
he set up: an online Australian Poetry Library.
          The sort of thing
a government should set up—no, not a government like
our government. But in an ideal world…

His poetry, I don't know. My taste & judgements
might be purely my own.

        The early work—
I mean, *The Blast Area, Crying in Early Infancy*

('The Pursuit
of the Modernist Heresy' in the form it took originally)—I liked
a lot.
I never wanted especially to write like him.

Under Berlin,
At the Florida were terribly 'assured'—& had really good poems
in them—and at this stage he must've seemed to most people to
be 'Mr Poetry'.

Work that could seem at the same time 'good' but 'not interesting'.

The licence John thought Post Modernism gave him
didn't produce good work. And the Ashbery Quest ditto.
But, again, these are my *opinions*—rather than
confidently held judgements. I'm likely wrong.
I'm not taken much with Ashbery after *Houseboat Days*—
& how can that be right?

Still, the 'terminals' are
not much fun to read.

Hard to write, granted.

John's even tone—unflappable control, urbane
sophistication—
seemed to rule out surprise or enthusiasm
or even genuine interest (I mean, *on his part*),
unless it was disguised. Did he ever or often
surprise himself? It might have been

that he was performing what he thought of as
the Master Writer Act, an impersonation, a
ticking of boxes?

Then — his too evident self regard.

Captain of the team, as one of us recently said?
Remember when it was mooted
there was a 'Tranter method', used
by the youngsters 'around' him?

                                            It *was* good to have him

counter Adamson's ecstasies
his will-to-swoon before fish.
Curious to see him
attempt to wish John Forbes
'back in the box', way too late.

A dinner at his & Lyn's (we went with J & S)—
where he derided, & chortled about, those he saw as losers
(people I had time for).

He can't have thought much of my writing—not early on: he
may have changed his mind.
Why *should* he have thought
much of my poetry, of course? No reason.

He tried to prove (not very successfully)
that he could 'do' each of Forbes, Laurie, &
Wearne.

My own two-facedness: but how, why,
            when would I tell him
how I saw things? I didn't know him well enough
to argue with him in a personal way.

                        And he clearly wasn't
down on me—
                especially, I think, after I'd declared
against Murray.

                    Before leaving Sydney I could
hardly get his attention. (And was lucky, maybe, in that.)
Once in Adelaide, I didn't need to deal with him.

The last few times I saw John—on trips here—he had
talked a lot—but not expected to listen much:

                            best to ignore
'the poor quality of our conversation', I think.

                        ('Hopeless,

these people don't know *any* good stories.')

It might also have been that he was losing hearing.
Cath & I had lunch with him in town & had to think,
after we had said goodbye, *Well, that was weird—as an*

experience: we had 'met the Author'. He was not unlikeable
on that occasion, but he had learned nothing about us.
He had seemed a little more vulnerable then,
but not by intention. Age, merely.

As will be the case,
with me, I know

I ought to read some of the poems again, to recall
the good ones—& see if there are others. Those
'Foucault at the Forest Lodge'-styled ones
won't be among them. (Except that, like much of his stuff,
the sentences are balanced perfectly, the weight falls exactly
on the words it should. He could write, he had intelligence
& the ability to work & concentrate.)

The product 'Australian Afternoon Tea' —

a weekender we stayed in
one time, had it. I liked the name, its suggestion
there was some notion current of an ('ideal')
Australian Afternoon: picture eucalyptus leaves
wattle, a shack or bungalow, a ute rusting
in long grass

—*'or here at the Metropole,'*

I think now—

        its ingenuously hopeful suggestion

of something quintessential:

            that,

               in an afternoon,

tea might precipitate

          not quite melancholy, but

something gentle, quiet—

            'bucolic', despite our

living in cities

          #

        Or 'leafily suburban'?

    #

Time to kick intellectual butt

    #

perhaps the traffic lightens or quickens,

the light is magically softer & still

               I get out

an anthology of Australian writing—dear to my

heart because I am in it

          a thing not very usual—

to see what Tranter's got in it, what

                    he's chosen

to be 'representative'

              and Jesus Christ! he starts out with

the 'Ode to Col Joye'

             a poem in my style——meant

as a riposte

         to jokes I made:

                  "As mag wheels are

to Tranter & the Beachboys / & as it is to breathe & swim

in the poetry of John Forbes"

        & the drawing of

'Alan Wearne & John Tranter as the aeroplane /

in that touching last scene from *Casablanca*'

\#

I like it because it has taken something of my style——

tho it has John's even, patient manner, exaggerated

for comic effect. How nice to have this, now, as endorsement

coming, as I do in the anthology, later.

                \#

                              Now the guy

                                        with the

small head

              like Leo G Carroll's

                              Dressed in black,

older than I am

                    but working 'in hospitality' ?

                              sits down

for an angry cigarette

                    twists his neck about,

                              changes tables

comes back, sits where he first sat

                              for ten minutes of

                                        an

Australian afternoon

                    #

                    Not that Leo G Carroll

                              if you remember

had a small head

                    #

gone, tho, somewhere, now, to kick some

butt

polish glasses

Night Thoughts

A painting I used to like a lot once & thought about

      I haven't thought about

      for some time. It showed

      Walter Benjamin at a table in Paris.

The artist's name I can't recall. Not Patrick—not Paul? Because,

the name that occurs to me is Patrick Caulfield—

      also minor—(much less

      varied—less ambitious,

      you might almost say).

This guy was South African, came to England, then

went to America—had some Jewish themes, painted

      even, a figure or two like

      Chagall. His colour

      too sweet too often. Not

'Peter'—what artist is called Peter (Peter

Paul Rubens, Peter Blake ... no-one I like).

      It strikes me,

      'He'd be right for Tranter'

      this artist—whose name

in a minute will come. 'Memes', a concept

that must have explained so much—or licensed it—

      for Tranter—who liked

      the elements, all, to be

      familiar—endorsed

by use, real because pre-existent. His talent

calling them up, in irresistible sequences: the

      hungry wives, the fizzy drinks,

      the smell of petrol, of meat—*of*

      meat, of course, *'sizzling'*—the colours of makeup,

of sunglasses, cocktails.   Cynicism then, affectlessness, appetite—

he liked all that. Real*ism* rather than reality—but

      who's going to argue? I mean, 'argue that'. (Now,

      'Actors' actors'—what about

      them? With a friend

I'd laugh: the duds—some*how*, some*where*—thus dubbed. George

Peppard. Richard Basehart. And a name I forget!

      Admittedly, Ben Gazzara

      finally became useful—

      long after Cassavetes had passed &

gone to heaven—useful older, playing old, annoying

stooges. Maybe he could play me? tho I am surely

      differently irritating.)

      Tranter 'could really write', that's

      the thing. Think: Fabulous Recreations

of Bad Film—so not *Mouchette*, but

Picnic. He liked the grammar? the screen syntax? the inevitable

      ordering of the known elements

      we saw & acknowledged quietly

      as awful—and banal, and, on

those grounds, Undeniable. (?) Was this 'scathing insight', was it

                       satire?

It was 'adult'. (So, 'memes'.) The phrase 'urban myth', tho it

      arrived as a cliché—

      with a clunk, use-value nil,

      work done—

claimed him: *Urban Myths*—his new & selected. What was

that artist's name now? whom-I-like tho-he's-

      limited?? (Where Caulfield

      is *all* limitations—but better,

      & I like him more, Caulfield—a technician.)

He retired somewhere weird, I think—walked every day half a mile for a Starbucks, read the paper, walked

        home again—to the studio. Worked.

        (Ben Gazzara as me?) (His

        name, I remember—(the artist's)—always raised

the problem of how to say it—which I'd

mastered. 'Established' it. When I remember it

        I'll say it.

        (The minor triumph

        or satisfaction, of pronouncing

Rooshay for Ruscha—*Skyler* for Schuyler … whom I'd called

Shyler for a while—& then *Shooler* for still longer.)

        (The poems survived.)

        'NIGHT THOUGHTS'.

        What else

have I been worrying at? Like a Guston character—

awake, staring down the barrel, thinking

        am I going to end my

        days critiquing Tranter?

        He's dead, he's gone.

Better tho, than making enemies among the young. Like

John, one wants to be loved.   'The Autumn of Central Paris'
>   is the painting's
>   title. Benjamin sits
>   surrounded by others,
at La Coupole or Les Deux Magots. We

know those zinc tables. Tranter would have. And
>   R. B. Kitaj, the artist
>   would have known them too—long
>   before he got to know Starbucks.
(Not a name, an initial —— 'R'. I would never have got there

saying Paul, Peter, Rhys or whatever.) I'd remembered the red in it.
>   It is an exhilaratingly
>   intelligent painting
>   a feeling of
'work done', in the compression of imagery & information—that
>   says

spies, fear, forces of Left & Right—the foreigners
>   —like Benjamin, who'd seen it
>   before—calculating,
>   taking the air, thinking *Paris*—
must get out soon. So much meaner than the Europe

Apollinaire mourned: shells sailing overhead—rain, cloud

—the 'Old' World represented

in the form of the Pope.

(Not totalitarianism, not much

'Ideology'.) So. I liked it—the Paris painting—

& took an interest in 'Kitarge' (pronounced

Kit-eye), that lapsed, tho I

liked his landscapes—of

Israel, Palestine). An artist *who thought a lot.*

(These are not 'worries'. I seem now, to be writing-for-fun.) 'Up

late',

as is said. As

I have said, often enough—my famous 'small mind'

given to repetition—calling

round the old sites,

checking for rust, broken pipes;

the papers the newsboy throws—that have built up

there by the tap; the leaking hose, its trail of green

where it feeds moss. But there

is no moss, no tap. (I sit in bed

writing this, seeing if I'll

think things I haven't thought before—or not quite

as I've thought them. I had a *list*. The third &

        final item a line of names

        that ended with a blank—a

        space for the name of Crab's

favourite *actors' actor*. I began the poem.) Time

would supply it, the name. And might. It hasn't yet.

        I did think, "A film—they could

        feature in. ... *Sci-fi?*"

        But they could not enhance

ANY movie. Why are women never considered actors' actors?

They can all act nowadays—might be the answer.

        Some I find

        irritating, but they can

        do the job, generally. Who

were the famous actresses 'of yesterday' who couldn't?

Susan Hayward, Jane Russell, others I suppose, and

        who cares? My friend,

        terminally ill: there is

        that to think about—tho I have

put it off for as long as possible ... so long foreshadowed.

'Ends'. Like Tranter's. My own, ... that can't be

    far off. Well, it can:

    but is it? The Great Night

    Worrier. Guston might be the

poster boy or talisman—that lonely worried head

a pillow behind—the round cheeks, the round eye

    focused on the ceiling,

    lost to its thoughts. (Is it

    smoking? as well? Maybe.)

'Martial Memories'—he came full circle—back to the

Works Project era. America's descent into

    mad self-delusion.

    (There is that to worry about, for me

    if not for Philip Guston.

I don't have much 'leverage' there exactly. Where 'exactly' do I have?)

Jesus Christ, 'Cliff Robertson'! I remember the actor.

    Well, no—but I find the list.

    As cardboard stands to mahogany

    so stands Cliff to ... whom really,

Marlon? Victor Mature? ELI WALLACH!

Lilli Palmer, maybe. Carey Mulligan. I can't really say
    "Who cares?" — I seem to.
    Philip Guston. I studied him
    along with the other Ab-Exers—
& liked him, his pulsing, slow abstracts. It was indicated

(Thank you, Terry) he was not as good as the real thing—
    Jackson, Bill,
    Mark Rothko,
    not even Motherwell.
The tides of fortune shifting just then,

the change of style—(rejected, then celebrated). His earlier work,
    of the 50s, 60s, seen suddenly
    as better too, in retrospect. (The corollary—
    now there's one you don't get
often 'in poetry'—of running down art by those deemed

unpleasant—the creeps—would be to extol art on the basis of
nice-guy,
    nice-woman status. There'd
    be difficult adjustments to make.
    Joan Mitchell—now was she an easy one
to be with? Independent, yes, fierce. But a charmer? Fun

to be around? O'Hara liked her. Twombly, for so long dudded,

  then flavour of the month—a sort

  of pastille that everyone could suck.

  Those sweet, sweet colours &

undemanding lines. If you *just got with it'* the things

were moving, ravishing, sophisticated—brutal ... savage.

  Ah! Life, Time, Desire,

  fine feelings—you could

  swoon if you wanted.

(You don't wanna swoon—what's wrong wit ya?)

Take it, or leave it. For a while we did. *An episode in*

  The history of Taste? Greenberg's

  one time phrase—

  applied, I think,

to Pop Art, or Minimalism. Bonnard had been so rapturously

received, in America in the 50s, the news had permeated

  here—& Terry

  (Thank you, Terry)

  could *see their point.*

We all could.

I can see it still. But, 'still', he's an uneven artist

     —figures sometimes flat,

     uncertain. Then great.

     Vuillard more consistent. Ruined

by his patrons. Court painter to a salon & a moneyed elite.

                      Marquet

—I don't know your work—really—but some I love.

     Reputations. I suppose it's

     mine I care about. But I 'don't have

     much leverage there',

do I? The Bobfish, Tranter, the dirigible Les—what will be

made of them? An enormous Murray figure, a Piccinini.

     I see it, floating, looking down

     on the suburb of Balmain—numerous

     Generation-of-68ers come out of

terraces, out of pubs & cafes, to stare at it—mouths tight—among

                      them

Tranter, his life blighted. Things have changed of course—

     something blander presides—

     a world of Best Australian Poems,

     ABR, the return of decorum, prizes.

Why so glum, pal? No reason—but how to end this stanza?

•

(They must end. But, once begun, why stop?

    Tho there is

    'Nothing to say'—'*and*

    Everything'.)

An *impression* of things—*a whole*—*given its adequate treatment*

(adjusted, allowed beam there, or sit occupying

    space, as it did) might

    have been Bonnard's

    ideal or intent—an

evenness—the cat the plate the table the lemon

the knife—the light & shadow—a kind of

    thin plenitude mildly stated

    precarious, but 'holding'—

    for one long moment. I am

recalling only one or two specific paintings

a memory. 'Specific' might be overstating it.

    But the yellow white & orange

    in just that balance I

    hope to see—& fear always

not to find—visiting Bonnard. A trip

to Melbourne then, maybe? (An exhibition, somewhere
              between famous & infamous,
              for its wallpaper.) 'Immersive'
              has been
the selling point of much I haven't liked the last few years—the

art reduced to spectacle, circus-ride, environment. No
              place for judgement. The Bonnards
              I like do something like that
              So much is brought
into balance—a long horizontal landscape of

hills, shallow valleys, roads, railway line, field &
              trees: pale greens, yellows, creams.
              Ochre. *Spots* (dabs) — of
              more intense colour — a work
of quietly spinning plates, tenuous but holding.

Like a spell, a moment. I wonder at Bonnard's
              mood then, was he tense
              or anxious—was their plenitude
              calming? (It's not Matisse,
or Monet or Pissarro. Not Vuillard, or Marquet—

all either decisive, or more *surface*—less equivocal,

        less troubled.) He had other

        interests, in his painting

        than this tenuous, populous equation,

but these are what I most love. Bonnard, you sweetie.

•

Hip & cool & tense, 'Blues For Elvin' plays

        as I drive, up the hills to

        the dentist at Blackwood

        feeling like I'm in a film:

scenes, in familiar firm pursuit—the hairpin turns

the twists & perilous cliffs, the guard rails

        as if I'm in the Mille Miglia

        the Targa Florio. *To Catch*

        a Thief? Two Weeks

In Another Town? numerous cheap 60s movies, set

in California, the West Coast—(a Corvette

        or Jag or Porsche, the Pacific

        beside, breakers rolling in, grass

        & sand dunes, the fence posts

catching light—*moon-light*—the sea dark

a heroine with scarf & hair in the wind

   Etcetera.) These movies

   never amounted to much.

   Freddy King comes on next—

making this definitely a teen movie & I

slow down, pull in, to the dentist's, park 'etcetera'.

   (Thank you, Lord B.) Cary Grant

   will remain known—

   for a few more years—running

regularly from that plane. Thru the wheat. His

eyebrows & business shirt, shoulders endearingly thin,

   cravat & clipped speech,

   flirting with Grace Kelly—

   the night, the sea, Monaco, the

fireworks scene—Hitchcock's joke about sex, its

dangerous thrill in the Hayes Era Imaginary.

   Ten more years?

   Historians—historians

   writing the History of Taste—

will remember him, as they do David Garrick,

or the greats of Shakespeare's moment. They are 'recorded':

   they can hardly be *remembered.*

   The frieze that crowns

   the Art Gallery of New South Wales—similarly—

'remembers' Praxitiles, Canova, Andrea del Sarto

Cimabue, Carracci—none now large in the mind

   of the casual punter

   calling in to see

   what gives in the

art world these days. Nothing much, pal. You see, it's

immersive you've got to give yourself *to* it—like the River Caves

   the Ghost Train or a

   light-show

   (Gape, if you can,

intelligently—your mind open.) But fulminating is easy.

And not to the point. Tho is having one

   my usual way? Don't I

   usually begin, & continue,

   pointless, blithe—'It

Serves Me Right To Suffer' ? No—'Glad To

Be Unhappy', a title that's always amused me

        tho the tune itself ...

        Eric Dolphy—always

        something of an enigma

(to me). Terry solved the provincialism problem

by going overseas—& becoming one of them

        The facts & innuendos

        the understandings he gave us

        —students in the 70s—

were fair enough. He was young himself. They were

the wisdom of the day. Terry Smith, handsome lecturer

        ambitious, 'political', ever-

        changing. The art changed too.

        By the time he got there

what remained? *October* magazine was lefter than he was. *Artforum*

was 'keeping up', not *calling the shots*—& Money

        was somehow ruining things

        'for everyone'. (Or did Koons

        come out okay?) Has wealth somehow

bought the artworld, so art can no longer stand aside—

the dais of high-minded reproof taken away? OK,

        down off the pedestal

        & entertain! When was

        the AGNSW opened, with its

pretence, or claim, of connection with the past,

or of continuity? Forlornly ridiculous—*none*

        of those artists

        is in the collection. Of course.

        "Go easy, mate."

There is art I like there: (Bonnard!)

Grace Crowley Wakelin Rollin Schlicht

        (who used to be my neighbour)

        a big Frank Stella, &

        a Morris Louis

that always hung beside it, tho it doesn't now

that inane graffito of a ship by Twombly

        there to keep the plebs

        in line with its inex-

        plicability. Lloyd

Rees. Ralph Balson's Artist-&-Model painting

of Crowley (or is it hers?) amusing & modern ... at the same
time.
   What else is great there?
   Kngwarreye. A picture with a
   bus ticket in it (real)
that struck me as a teenager. I was in there out

of the rain. I next went back some years later
   primed—thank you, Terry—
   armed with the taste of
   my time—inured to all surprise. My
teeth are fine, says Shelly. So I must not be grinding them.

•

The figure, a small dark upright accent, out there
   on the pontoon, might be
   Stewart MacFarlane returned
   to the site of his
doomy-est work. An artist whose reputation

goes up & down while the work gets better & better.
   The reputation
   unrevised—but
   shelved, forgotten. I saw
his work, aspects of it, in Fairfield Porter—an

influence MacFarlane wouldn't hide: in fact, I failed

> to understand when he

> first mentioned it—

> but I hadn't seen

as much of Porter as I should have (Porter, too,

… better than I'd allowed). *Was everybody*

> *nice about him*

> *as a* 'decent chap'—

> (or the American equivalent)?

No. 'Great'—tho behind the march of events. Again,

Bonnard, Vuillard, Jane Freilicher. Porter. Cath

> went down for a swim came

> back. No Stewart MacFarlane?

> I don't ask of course. Where

is he now? Where am I—Port Elliot, *in bed,*

reading, the kids, Max & Finn, barely audible on the

> floor above, their

> mother finishing the

> jigsaw puzzle we all

laboured at after dinner—*my head* in part, '*in*

this novel. ('Italy'—an author so concerned with it

    the plot stops every

    paragraph

    for description—linen,

furnishings, the birds, the arrangement of rooms, the

ease of the those behind the counter *where the coffee*

    can be ordered, & where

    one—the heroine—

    reaps endorsement from

the proprietor—received as a kind of blessing the Italian

knows is anticipated & must be conferred on the Englishwoman—

    she'd be crushed were it omitted.

    A tourist

    knows the feeling, even

a northerner, like myself, from South Australia.) (To take

some perspective on this: E.M. Forster, Tranter, me—

    Christobel Kent—*A Party*

    in San Niccolo.) Cath swims

    in Horseshoe Bay, *will* again

tomorrow—as we 'leave'—& visit one more time, with Anna,

                         Chris,

the kids—Finn-the-Fierce & Max, cool-&-brave. Will they ever think

       of Stewart MacFarlane? The odds

       it seems are against it. He could

       paint them there tho, at Horseshoe Bay,

precarious—as I never want to see them be. I love them.

An Unsuitable Attachment

> "You were all I ever dreamed of"
>
> — girl on bus

> "Lonely are the Brave"
>
> — graffiti, in Glebe, Sydney

So there you sit, at the Metropole, no
       your usual table—
       in the sunlight, that will fall
       in this spot a few minutes,
—the Lapin Agile—whose lone

barman, used to your presence, will shortly bring
       coffee, a brioche
       but in his own good time
       as you are early
'ahead of yourself' (to whom you mean

to catch up), an unlikely advertisement for the new:
       French, no-one more so,
       but not quite French—
       some Italian, some Greek
a good dash of Poland. A citizen. With a *review*

in mind—what could be *more* French?—to write, or propose.

An article, a statement of

principles. But which?

Not Marinetti's ('the

caffeine of Europe'). Happy to disclose,

as if tentatively, out the corner of your mouth, *an indication*—

because these things are

'hard to say'—of the new formulation

that is 'in the air', you will imply.

A feeling, a shared mood, working its way

to a decisive, imminent, certain turn. As if

the avant-garde

are deer, testing the breeze—

tho they don't know it,

'about to move'. Picabia, Picasso, Derain, Braque, loopy

de La Fresnaye, Robert Delaunay. A gathering movement,

fresh as yet.

Unstable.

Your tone will be intimate,

familiar: you are a writer—cheerful, instinctive your feel for change, your taste. The new order is certain. With

     your verses you are

     its proof. Their

     nonchalance, their decision,

their 'swift elisions'. Your account—as if you look into yourself

and gauge these moments. The 'now', the future,

     how it will be.

     Rueful, tender, un-

     formed—but

nascent—& in the atmosphere that, of course, you breathe.

How to begin? A two-part publication—there is

     money for it. Picabia's.

     You will write it.

     How begin? *Begin*

as if these things are tentative & subtle: as yet

so new—a thing latent, about to gel, declare

     a nature it can hardly

     know as yet. Decisive moves

     from one or another

and the tide will turn. One says this with a certain

nonchalance. The Spaniards—Juan Gris, Pablo—the

       'not quite French'—

       might be the key. Picabia.

       What is the buzz.

Modigliani, Kupka. Sonia. Marie Laurencin? Is

Derain modern anymore, or Matisse? What words

       can gather them,

       summon their character?

       But it's 1914

Later than you think—& some months afterwards

you are sitting near your tent, the night air cool, & still.

       Huge shells tear thru it

       from somewhere distant to

       somewhere far away. Low cloud

across the sky, silver in the moonlight, the

empty fields are dark. Europe. One single farmhouse

       showing a light. A thump

       & earth & mud in

       clumps fall about you

or rain down. The Future shows up, with its new machinery

                      —of which

the Pope can hardly approve—& gives you freedom, excitement.

> The Future, in
>
> Apollinaire's case,
>
> whacks you about the head.

(This is it. Do you hear?) Cubism might have suddenly seemed

less 'of the moment'. (Like the Pope. Like Maurice Denis.) It is

> a different moment now.

#

The Paris of the past—his past. Pre-war—post-war.

> To be back, 1918, the same
>
> zinc metal table, same coffee.
>
> Modernity—had it come?

Had it gone? Everyone was in town.

It felt different. What was he leader *of*? Some had not returned.

> Some—Tzara, Duchamp—
>
> seemed not to take things
>
> seriously, or were newly serious. Different.

Is this *serious History*? It can't be. It can't be just a roll-call, though it must at least be that. I can just about recall

   what 1986 felt like—

   (to me)—my narrow focus being

   exactly these things.

A photo of me & Dave Glazbrook outside Al Fresco's

comically earnest looking, but also—in my case—bizarre:

   my hair enormously cantilevered

   with hair gel, wildly curled

   & blonded, while I wear

a tight leather jacket, a curious combination the times

would allow, but not mandate. I suppose I was happy—

   unselfconscious

   tho I am rarely so

   I thought about Apollinaire

even then, as I had for years, & Manet, *Les Demoiselles,*

Johns & Rauschenberg, Stella, Morris Louis, Sol LeWitt, the

           Conceptualists,

   the Post-Object crowd.

   (Kosuth, *Art & Text.*)

   Kiefer & the Germans. Ryman.

The artists I knew were interesting: Shaun & Bronwyn,

          Andy P & others.

Micky Allan. Linda & Paul. Richard. Kerin Murray.

> Apollinaire's world

> (or Frank O'Hara's)

> —microcosms, focal points.

'Like Adelaide'—a joke I could always make. The

Provincialism Problem. The essay of that name

> made Terry Smith the

> unpopular bearer

> of bad news. (He published it

in *Artforum*—the only way to get ahead—neatly illustrating

his own thesis. An irony, of course. Nevertheless

> it seemed true.

> It still does.)

> My own fascination

with the old centres plainly the childish wish

to *know what it felt like*. Endless, rarely conclusive detail

> or context, might

> get you there,

> tho never demonstrably.

Long periods go by where I never think about it

Then some find will have me hoover it up. (Was the vacuum-cleaner

    named after

    the President? I forget

    which were the good ones.

There were not so many. Anyway, I meant mainly to wonder—

        briefly—

if "hoover" still functioned as a verb these days?) Then

    I would go on

    to something else. *A*

    Tour About The Estate—

was a Kingsley Amis title I always thought funny. Is my mind

a kind of 'estate'? "But anyway"—just let me add—so we can

    'move on'—& maybe give these

    single quote marks a rest.

    Tho for how 'long', ha ha.

We don't want more of Paris, Apollinaire, Cendrars

Manet, Victorine Meurent, what somebody said to somebody else—

    Marie Laurencin, Mina Loy.

    Actually, the Germans I always

    find sympathetic

because they —like us— feel barred from the centres. Paris, at least. Heckel & Kirchner, Beckmann, the nuts

      of the seventies & later—

      Oehlen, for me, for now, the

      ne plus ultra—

Sigmar Polke, Kippenberger. Art history, as it writhes & convulses.

      If that's what it does.

\#

The fifties & sixties—in art at least—I don't mean rock & roll—

      I feel close enough to

      to not be curious. I 'know'

      how it'd have felt

for Rauschenberg when he did those white canvases at Black Mountain.

If the others were incredulous around him—*that*

      I don't understand.

      And Johns's paintings

      like 'Good Time Charley'

I'd have loved to have done, for exactly his reasons

I know I didn't have to work my way to these

      & didn't make them—

      but in 1970 I saw the point

      I was 'on board'. (As

who wasn't, I guess, by then?) Favourite lines—transcribed—of someone's criticism—I have come across again: I love them still.

      (Not Greenberg's. Rosen-

      berg's? Lucy Lippard's?)

      To quote,

"Judd's, Morris's, Andre's, Steiner's, some but not all of Smithson's,

some but not all of LeWitt's" — *and* — "For every genuine moment in

      modern sculpture—such as John

      Chamberlain's own

      crushed-automobile sculptures

of the mid-fifties—there are hundreds & hundreds of driftwood vulvas,

cast in bronze & called *Departure*." (The artists' names, a list of things-

      approved. Note all the possessives.)

      (Minimalists. But whose list?

      And is it Ashbery? or

O'Hara? the line about driftwood? Lippard for the long list

is my bet—maybe Ashbery for the driftwood joke.) Greenberg—

                            his writing

      I thought admirable, terrific

      it had such weight

      Wrong, finally,

when he made to enforce a particular direction. (He succeeded for a time.)

And then the art world had to roll it back, his opinions, his dicta.

      Schjeldahl is very good

      on the marooned archi-

      pelago of rich-man's good taste

that the large abstracts he advocated have become—

Mandarin—meaningless markers of social caste, success

        & self-endorsement—acres

      of Olitski & Noland

      in vast rooms in the

Hamptons: pastel-clad drinkers, drink in hand, contemplating them

(or the landscape—out of identically long windows: beach & sea &

      horizon.) What I really wonder about—

      would like to know—

      What was it like, exactly,

when he introduced the boys to Frankenthaler's new move?

Did he indicate, in so many words, "This is it. Go for it.

      Get there

      before she does"?

      And she had been

his girlfriend. Olitski, Noland, Morris Louis

were gifted this stain technique & its meaning made clear to them

What a tip—

that they took. Later,

the studio visits

where Greenberg would indicate where some endless length of

canvas should be cut & the stooge would dutifully wander off, find

the scissors. You don't

argue with the master.

His chutzpah

in the early writing. Later, the bullying tough-guy nastiness.

I was struck by his handsome resemblance

to Telly Savalas

which seems appropriate.

The tales of his

punching people. The sniggering leader-of-the-gang labelling,

of unfavoured painters, as 'stinkers'. Who laughed?

Who—nervous—thought

"I'm next"? the ostracising

of Philip Guston (&

others who'd changed to names less Jewish)—for

breaking ranks. Some of the writing was great

     'Avant-Garde & Kitsch'

     is important. The standard

     of American criticism

lifted after Greenberg, his example & principles formalised—

as art writing became professional, institutionalised, taught.

     (Some of that killer-instinct

     continued—probably still

     has—*Artforum*'s unstated

early rules included *No figurative painters, only abstract*

(no matter how good / how bad)—*Never cover any movement's*

     second generation. This lasted

     for decades.) I'd have

     understood Larry Rivers painting

George Washington, thinking 'This is so wrong—so dopey, so

                     uncalled for—

it has to be right. It's funny sure enough. I must call Frank.'

            Laughing. Like delivering

     a shaggy-dog joke

     to the court of

     Serious Opinion.

The affront & incomprehension that would eventuate—

a success de ('du'?) scandal. (My inner life a matter of identifications

       with moments-of-the-past—all

       imagined. *What a life.*)

       There are some jokes here too

in these notebooks. (Not all jokes.) "Toulouse-Lautrec had short legs,

I have a short neck. Our burden." & *"Haiku:* Alan Jeffries meets

       John Forbes—main street—Mildura.

       The Shock Of The New"

       More sensitively

"If only you could be a girl for a little while and, moreover,

such a peculiar one as I ..." — letter, Jenny Von Westphalen

       to Karl Marx. "My life,

       which seems so

       monotonous" (Jean Rhys) "is really

a complicated affair, of cafes where they like me & cafes

where they don't, streets that are friendly, streets that aren't, rooms

       where I might be happy, rooms

       where I never shall be, looking glasses

       I look nice in," etcetera. Jean Rhys.

Kerouac—on the other hand—died watching The Galloping Gourmet.

"… tho laughter / Leaves us so doubly serious shortly after"

—Byron, *Beppo*, LXXIX

"Poetry

is the clear expression

of mixed feelings" —Auden.

(I hope I make myself clear. And you can see where this is headed.) "I,

even as the dogs, feel the need for the infinite" &

there you are,

attractive, on the

bear skin rug of

my heart.   Don't be afeared.   "Balance, largeness, precision,

contempt for nature

in all its particularity — that is the great & absent art of our age."

Thank you, Clement.) (I guess

if you had wanted

'incident'

you could look out that window.) A strange idea

that painting should *have* none—were they to be

a step up from

'Matisse-&-

the-armchair'—a sort of

anaesthetic? ("Acres & acres of expressionless kitsch.") Lippard held that Olitskis were "visual muzak". Peter Schjeldahl thought

    Frankenthaler an artist

     "of maximum pretension &

     minimum vitality",

of "little ideas" given "great size"——over rating, & over rated for,

                                        'restraint'.

Not me. Not me I think. Not my good intentions! I mean, Ideas,

    & Size——

     but not rated highly enough

     to be over rated.

Cath & Pontoon At Horseshoe Bay

Streaking black dogs on the beach,
two of them. Black are the best,

                    witty & French

like illustrations

Cath at the other end

The sun bronzing her skin

Still a shadow—from the low sun out at sea—

    giving her

              and the rocks

    definition

              Sort of thing

a bad painter would love

But great in real life

The little un-romantic pontoon

      floats

          like a lozenge

Happily bouncing about

                          Cath, now,

Between the beach and it

                Plunges and swims.

                          God,

What a giant sky—white

        out on the horizon,

with cloud that seems quite close, but can't be

And then blue,

           that darkens, as your eye travels 'up'

           to one small whiskery whirl of cloud—

           and is actually not very dark

Just cheery

Way down on the right are the splashes Cath makes

over by the jetty

           and she stands,

back in the shallows, where the beach rounds

on the sea.

The eye zips leftwards

    following the breakwater

                  Skips further

And there further down
Is the happy little lozenge

      Like a pat of butter

     (in white protective foil)

Or an after-dinner mint

      Floating about

      A domino

      In the middle ground.

    Cath,
I think,

    Has gone up the stairs
to wash off the sand, dry

    and change

And we'll set off back. But no.

Here she is,

       towelling her hair.

            Coffee?
            It's on the cards

            But unlikely
            What a day

Notes

◊ *Ben Sando Ode*—Ben Sando, artist. Ira Hayes—celebrated as symbol but, as an individual, ignored by the Great Society.

◊ *('If you take requests') The Stars*—Sam Cooke, 'Having A Party': "If you take requests I've got a few for you / play that song called 'Soul Twist', play that one called 'I Know' … no other songs will do."

◊ *Swimmeroonie*—intrigued by Mathews' poem 'The Swimmer' I tried many times to produce an equivalent. The best lines here are those borrowed from his original, more or less plagiarism.

◊ *Kate* — a poem that began with no focus—until my friend's phone brought the news of Kate Jennings' having died. This is not a balanced appraisal. She was great.

◊ *Midwinter Day*—The title of Bernadette Mayer's book-length poem. A *Poetry Says* podcast deals with it.

◊ *A Misty Day in Late July, 2020*—Covid, 'the contagion', as experienced by Adelaide: a 'phoney war' situation, as the city at the time remained relatively disease-free. The epigraph is from Shirley Hazzard.

◊ *Oh Boy Bear and Berrigan*—a bear drawn for a grandchild. Ted Berrigan's *So Going Around Cities* had its back cover facing up as I wrote—with his photo on it. The poem's question, What were they doing?—Bronwyn was in London, Crab had broken his arm (hence 'lying down'), Ben was in Melbourne. 'Yeti'?—mine turned out more bearish. Photo of Berrigan—by Alain.

◊ *An Australian Afternoon* deals (like *Night Thoughts*) with ideas about the work of John Tranter: he had recently died & this sent me back to the poems, tho 'back' is hardly right—I had not paid attention for a few decades or more. I was surprised at my own response. Some details: 'Ode to Col Joye' is very kind as a riposte. It relates most to my poem 'Water'. I look now at other of Tranter's poems & find many to like, among them the Foucault poem •

The 'other John' mentioned was John Jenkins • The Terminals: a form John Tranter invented & which occupied him for some time • *Houseboat Days* is a John Ashbery collection from 1977 • Leo

G. Carroll—obscure in the 2020s, if he ever was not obscure, a minor actor now best remembered as the Intelligence chief in Hitchcock's *North by Northwest* & by the elderly as the boss, 'M', in TV's *The Man from U.N.C.L.E.*. The pub, the Metropole, is in fact the Metropolitan.
• There are references to Australian poetry & to details & events that might be regarded now as minutiae: viz 'Rimbaud & the Pursuit of the Modernist Heresy' *as it appeared* in *New Poetry* magazine, the title of a Tranter poem I read a lot once; & poets Robert Adamson & Les Murray, they loomed large in their time. The anthology referred to—*Macquarie PEN Anthology of Australian Literature.*
◊ *Night Thoughts*—I've liked a good number of John Tranter poems just recently: 'Lufthansa', 'Paradise' among them. 'The Beach' is another—capacious, a long & baggy hold-all built on the 'sestina-principle' to contain ... *everything.* There are others. Poets, in any case, are remembered for their best poems. One poet is remembered for poems about eating curries & wearing short pants • R.B. Kitaj—an interesting painter, an American: I don't know why I thought South African. I do know I regarded it as fact for a long while. Kitaj was an important part, in the 1960s, of the London scene—from which he later became alienated • Terry Smith—art historian, curator. 'The Provincialism Problem' is the title of his essay diagnosing, correctly, the relationship of Australian Art to that elsewhere, America chiefly. Its message was much resisted • 'Martial Memory', an early work by Guston • The Bobfish—a friend's nickname for Robert Adamson • "a life blighted": Tranter once complained of his misfortune in writing during the reign of Les Murray • Christobel Kent, *A Party in San Niccolo*, the book read in Port Elliot • Stewart MacFarlane: an Australian painter with a career in America & in various parts of Australia. His subjects are usually dramatic & intense, often showing people isolated, troubled, trapped, resigned or desperate. They are serious & yet ironic & often formally very powerful. The landscapes sad but beautiful. 'Unease' is a quality he tries for. [*From an earlier draft, given here as prose*: "The melodrama that might place Tranter's poems in some world of pulp fiction, graphic novel—unserious, foolish even, scenarios & images pre-used—should tell against MacFarlane's

paintings. It doesn't. *But the comparison indicates we might consider Tranter as Pop?* an equivalent of Lichtenstein or Rosenquist? This doesn't feel right." And in fact I don't like considering MacFarlane that way either.] • The stanza form derives from Tranter's poem 'Journey' which, additionally, has each first & last line rhyme.

◊ *An Unsuitablee Attachment* — thoughts about 'moves', *movements*, career paths, influence, patterns of change within the arts. Some details: Marinetti claimed he was "the caffeine of Europe" • Picabia was to fund a second Apollinaire essay introducing 'the new'. It was to have included much reference to him • I compress a decade or so of Apollinaire's life into a seemingly shorter span • "The pope can hardly approve"—see the lines in *Alcools* bringing together the Pope and the wondrous modernity of cannons etc to give a picture of Europe • "The artists I knew" at the time, & thru the 90s: Shaun Kirby, Bronwyn Platten, Linda Marie Walker & Paul Hewson, Micky Allan, Andrew Petrusevics, Richard Grayson, Kerin Murray are those mentioned • *A Tour About the Estate*—a Selected Poems volume by Kingsley Amis • Victorine Meurent modelled for Manet. She was herself a painter • "I'd have loved to have done, for exactly his reasons"—this is ridiculous, I realise • Helen Frankenthaler. "Get there before she does." What do I know? But I bet he thought only a male artist could make it count. He understood what she was doing—so it was his, he could give it away • Telly Savalas played a loveable Brooklyn-accented TV detective in the 70s. He looked a little like Greenberg • *Artforum*'s unspoken but firm policies— see *Challenging Art: Artforum 1962—1974* by Amy Newman • Amongst the lines of criticism I found in my notebooks— transcribed for the fun of them—were also jokes & scribblings of my own: *viz* the Lautrec ditty. And the Haiku. Followed by—well, the poem tells it—a quoted letter, lines from Jean Rhys. • Readers of John Forbes will hear the line "Acres of expressionist kitsch"— from his poem 'Europe—a guide'. Along with "Not me—not my good intentions!"